INTRODUCTION

Happy children have positive attitudes about themselves and others that impact the way they cope with stress, changes, relationships, and other challenges they will encounter as they grow to adulthood. In order for children to develop positive attitudes about themselves, they need a strong self-image, which depends upon feeling both lovable and capable.

Feeling lovable has to do with traits that are unique to your child's personality, such as a sense of humor, creativity, friendliness, or perseverance. Children feel lovable when they know that they are appreciated for who they are and not for what they have achieved.

Feeling capable has to do with behaviors that are more like skills, such as being able to listen and follow directions; feeling good about washing, dressing, and getting ready for bed independently; having a sense of who you are and what your limitations might be; and knowing how to be safe and healthy. Children feel capable when they are given the freedom and encouragement to develop at their own pace, make mistakes, and achieve the goals they set for themselves.

Your child's self-image and well-being must be positively reinforced every day. As you read *Raising Happy Kids*, reflect on the ways that you communicate with and respond to your child on a daily basis.

The more aware you become of how your actions and examples affect your child's emotional life, the easier it will be for you to provide him or her with an environment that is truly capable of nurturing a happy, well-adjusted child.

A Word About Safety: The activities in *Raising Happy Kids* are appropriate for young children between the ages of 3 and 5. However, keep in mind that if a project calls for using small objects, an adult should supervise at all times to make sure that children do not put the objects in their mouths. It is recommended that you use art materials that are specifically labeled as safe for children unless the materials are to be used only by an adult.

CONTENTS

Feeling Loved

Messages

The heart shape can show up in many ways that say "I love you."

Caring messages that show up in surprising places and times will make your child feel special.

- With sidewalk chalk, draw a heart with his name in it in front of your home.
- Put heart stickers on notepaper, and safety-pin the paper to his pillow or slip it under his cereal bowl.
- Send your child a letter or a postcard just for fun. Help him discover the letter in the mail, and then read it to him.
- Make a cardboard frame for a picture of your child. Decorate it with heart-shaped candy and display it on a family bulletin board.

Special Days

Birthdays and holidays can seem far apart to a young child.

Everyone needs special days to look forward to throughout the year. Designating one day every month as your child's special day is a great way to break out of the routine and show your love. The special day should bring special privileges that you and your child agree on and plan for ahead of time, such as choosing a family game to play, having a friend over, taking a short trip, eating a picnic lunch, planning the day's menu, dressing up, staying up an extra hour, watching favorite videos, or making dessert.

Touch

A spontaneous, unexpected hug or kiss means a lot.

Nothing beats the power of touch for dispelling fears, frustration, and sadness. Showing your child that he is a huggable, kissable, lovable person will go a long way in helping him gain a positive outlook on life and build self-esteem. Cuddling, hair ruffling, and holding hands are just a few great ways to communicate your love.

Try to touch your child lovingly each day. Make it easier for him to communicate his need for affection by keeping a "hug jar" filled with heart-shaped notes. When he gives you a heart, it means he needs a hug.

Surprise Gifts

Presents are as much fun to open as to receive what's inside.

Once in a while, give a simple, tiny gift to your child as a surprise, even if it's not her birthday or a holiday.

Wrap it and tag it with her name. The surprise can be a candy kiss, a special fruit, a small book, some crayons, a flower bouquet, or even a pretty shell or stone. It's the message that counts, not the size or value of the surprise.

Secret Signals

Signing "I love you" is a fun and simple way to show your child you care.

Children respond to body language much more readily than words. Develop a secret signal to use with your child that means "I love you." This might be a tug on one ear, a thumbs-up signal, a wink, a blink, a hand squeeze, or the gesture for "I love you" in sign language. (Extend your thumb, index finger, and pinkie while bending down your two middle fingers.) Send your love via your secret signal whenever the opportunity arises, and encourage your child to use the secret signal, too. The following are great times to use your secret signal.

- In a doctor's or a dentist's office
- At the airport
- On bus or car rides that seem too long
- While talking to someone on the phone
- When your child "takes a back seat" to visitors
- When you're both tired but have errands to run
- To say goodbye at school

Notice and Share

Teach your child every day that he is special.

When you notice traits and behaviors that are special and unique to your child, share them with him, taking the time to be specific. Compliments such as the following help to reinforce the message that your child's specialness has a positive effect on the people around him.

- "No one else has the same special twinkle that you have in your eyes."
- "I don't know anyone else who notices how the plants and flowers in our yard change every day. You are a really good observer."
- "No one giggles the way that you do. Your laugh is contagious. Just hearing you laugh makes me laugh, too."
- "When you listen, you look right into the eyes of the person who is talking. You are a really good listener, and that is a very special gift."

Tapes

Preserve your child's precious moments for years to come.

Your child will change and grow quickly, but technology has made it easier to preserve many precious moments in your child's life. Show your child that you value her by tape-recording her voice. Capture her candidly while conversing or telling a story, or have a recording session for her to recite her favorite nursery rhymes and sing her favorite songs. Date the tape and add to it at least once a year.

If you have access to a video camera, videotape your child regularly. Capturing holidays and special events is exciting, but don't stop there. Film your child's everyday activities such as telling you about her paintings or drawings. Film her as she feeds a pet, helps sort the laundry, plays dress up, makes cookies, or plays with family and friends.

Make it Easy to Be Clean

Child-inspired products such as animal-shaped bath mitts, bright-colored hairbrushes, and soap crayons keep grooming activities fun.

Children have a natural interest in their body and what they can do with it. Every day, do at least one small thing that shows your child that his body is important. Help him learn how to keep his body clean, fit, and protected from both disease and the elements. Teach him to "tune in" and be aware of the care that his body needs. The following are suggestions for making it easy for your child to stay clean.

- Put a step stool near the sink, and keep small towels within reach.
- Let him have his own set of towels in his favorite color or personalized with his initials.
- Use liquid soap dispensers, which are easier to handle than slippery bars of soap.
- Let him use baby oil or lotion on his skin to make it soft and sweet-smelling.
- Use shampoo that does not burn the eyes.
- Make sure he washes his hands with soap after toileting and before every snack or meal.

Germs

Periodically, clean your child's toys with a bleach and water solution and opt for washable dolls and stuffed animals.

Use a spray bottle to show your child how germs travel in the air just like a fine spray of water. Tell her that germs are too small to see, and that many germs could fit inside one drop of water. Let her know that germs make people sick, and that we use soap and medicines to kill them and prevent them from spreading. Coughing, sneezing, and touching things with dirty hands are all ways that people spread germs to others. Consider the following disease prevention tips.

- Have her try to keep fingers clean and away from her eyes, nose, and mouth.
- Show your child the proper way to sneeze or cough into a tissue, and encourage the habit of throwing it in the garbage can right away.
- If no tissue is available, teach your child how to lift an arm and sneeze or cough into her shoulder.
- Discourage the habit of sharing drinking glasses and plates while eating.

Fear of Doctors

Knowing what to expect during a visit will ease your child's anxiety about seeing her doctor.

Prepare your child before a checkup by reading books about going to the doctor or explaining what a doctor does and why it is important for her to be seen by one. With your doctor's permission, take your child to the office just to familiarize her with the building and play with the toys in the reception room. Let her meet the doctor as a friend without the stress of an examination. Reassure her that as a friend, the doctor wants to help her stay well.

Another way to prepare your child for a visit to the doctor is to role-play many of the things that will happen. Have fun and be positive as you pretend the following.

- Weigh her and measure her height.
- Use a mini-flashlight and tongue depressor to look at her throat and ears.
- Feel her neck as if checking for lumps.
- Tap her kneecap to test her reflexes.
- Listen to her heart and lungs with a toy stethoscope.

Eating Right

Set a good example for your child through your own healthy eating habits.

Plant the seeds for healthy lifetime eating habits by providing your child with healthy foods for mealtimes and snacktimes. Give her fun experiences with healthy foods by letting her scrub or cut up fruits and vegetables to keep handy for snacks. Show her how to prepare simple dips with salad dressing mix and plain yogurt or cottage cheese. Let her dip fresh vegetables in peanut butter or melted cheese. Purchase sugarless cereals and whole grain crackers and breads. Make simple desserts from fresh fruits.

Serve balanced meals at regular times, and make them a pleasant, unhurried family time. Encourage your child to try new foods and to chew slowly and completely before swallowing. Make sure that she drinks plenty of water each day. A special plastic glass or funny ice cube molds will increase her interest in drinking water.

Tooth or Consequences

Most dental problems can be prevented by teaching your child good dental health habits.

Keeping your child's baby teeth healthy will ensure strong, healthy permanent teeth. Your child will brush best when you are there with him, modeling. Give him his own small tube of toothpaste and a soft-bristled toothbrush, and encourage the habit of brushing teeth after meals and before bedtime. Show him the right way to use his toothbrush to gently reach all of his teeth and scrub them in a circular motion. By the time children are 3, they can also begin to floss their teeth with minimal help.

Sweets and sugared cereals are obvious cavity makers. But also keep in mind that even fruit juices and milk contain sugars that can damage teeth. One of the major causes of tooth decay in young children is letting a toddler carry a bottle filled with juice or milk and suck on it at will. If possible, try to wean your child from a bottle before his first birthday. If your child sleeps with a bottle, or uses it as a security object, keeping it filled with water will not damage his teeth.

Stress Busters

Music and laughter can positively transform your child's life.

Incorporate humor into daily life with funny stories, books, and planned surprises. Humor will help you and your child stay in balance, and keep life's adversities in perspective. Encourage your child's sense of humor by noticing and responding to his jokes and funniness. Surprise your child with your sense of fun whenever possible. If he is pouty or angry, get out a pot, put it on your head, and sit on the counter. Use his laughter to break the tension, and then talk about what's bothering him in a calm, clear way that respects his feelings. But be careful that you don't belittle him or his feelings. Try to risk being funny or spontaneous even if spontaneity doesn't come naturally to you, and encourage your child to risk being silly himself.

Music is another great way for everyone in your family to reduce stress, recharge, and maintain a healthy emotional balance. Use music in your home to create moods of joy, vitality, peace, or relaxation. Share music with your child while you work around the house, exercise, or prepare for naps or bedtimes. Children who enjoy making and listening to music find that it helps them release their aggressive or negative feelings and stay positive. Using pots, pans, and other household items, make simple instruments for your child such as shakers, drums, and cymbals. Or purchase them inexpensively from toy stores. If your child demonstrates a true interest in music or dance, encouraging this talent will have lifelong benefits.

Journals

Focusing on emotional fitness is just as important as keeping physically fit.

Many people find that the best way for them to maintain balance and emotional fitness is to write out their feelings and thoughts in a daily personal journal. This is such an important avenue for keeping emotionally fit that parents should encourage its beginnings during the preschool years. Your child cannot yet write words about her thoughts and feelings, but you can. Provide her with blank books or scrapbooks and encourage her to tell you a little about her day or her feelings about it. Try to write in the journal almost every day.

Keep it simple. Do not expect more than a sentence. Give your child the option of making a drawing to express herself instead of using words, or of illustrating what you have written for her. Always remember that you are encouraging a wellness habit and not a diary or an original manuscript.

Photos

A picture is worth a thousand words.

No one else looks just like your child, and a photograph of your child alone, with the rest of the family, or with friends will make your child feel proud and loved. Creatively displaying photographs of your child throughout your home is a great way to show her how unique she is, and make her feel special at the same time. Here are just a few ideas to try.

- Have a favorite candid photo of your child enlarged to poster size and hang it in her room or your family room.
- Take "funny face" pictures together in an arcade booth and use them to decorate your refrigerator.
- Get a special frame that holds several pictures at once, and add a new photo of your child each year to show how she has changed. Or use one picture frame and put the new photo over the old one each year.
- Tape your child's photo to the center of a play dollar bill (such as the play dollars used in the board game Monopoly) and make multiple copies of the play money for use in pretend play and sorting games.

Outgrowing

Teach your child about sharing the clothes he has outgrown.

Save just a few of your child's outfits, shirts, or shoes as they are outgrown. Be sure to save his baby shoes! When you do your annual closet and drawer cleaning, involve your child. Show him the clothes or the shoes he has outgrown, and have him compare them to his current ones. Your child will take pleasure in this visual evidence of his physical growth.

Mirrors

Self-acceptance is all-important for children of all ages.

It's as important to your child's self-esteem to learn to say something good about herself every day as it is to learn to accept the compliments of others. Make it easy for your child to admire her reflection by giving her a child-safe hand mirror, hanging a full-length mirror in her bedroom, or making sure that some of the mirrors in your home are hung at her eye level. Provide a stepladder or a stool so that she can climb up and look at herself in your mirror with you. Point out how many teeth she has, what color her eyes are, and how grown-up she looks in her new clothes. Help her appreciate and express pleasure in her own appearance by asking questions such as the following.

- "Do you like your little smile? Your great big smile?"
- "Can you see your dimple?"
- "Do you like what you chose to wear today?"
- "What do you see that you like about yourself?"

Your Child's Name

Your child's name is a symbol of herself and her uniqueness.

Whether you picked your child's name out of a name book or chose to honor a favorite friend or relative, your child will enjoy knowing the history of her name. Make her name special to her by celebrating it in the following ways.

- Put her name and date on every art project.
- Add her name to food by dripping pancake batter to form her initials, using candy sprinkles to put her name on cupcakes, or writing her name with catsup or mustard on sandwiches.
- Name some of her favorite foods or cookies after her.
- Keep a personalized folder for her drawings, dictated stories, and creations.

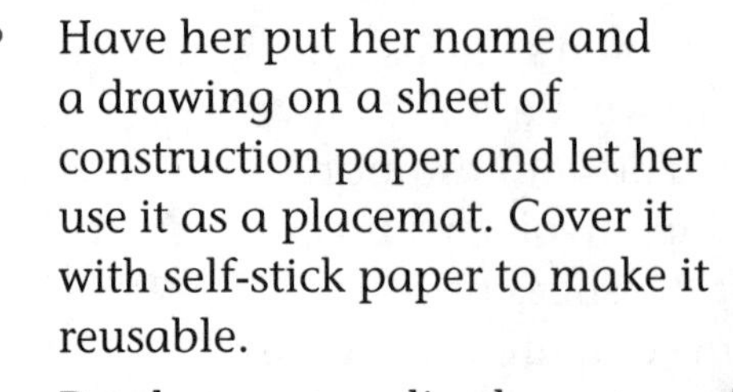

- Have her put her name and a drawing on a sheet of construction paper and let her use it as a placemat. Cover it with self-stick paper to make it reusable.

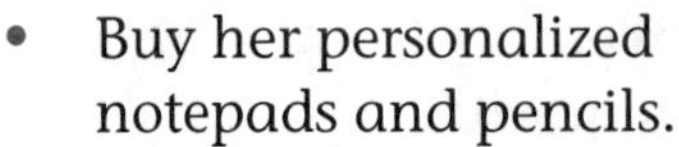

- Buy her personalized notepads and pencils.

Coloring

Physical differences are interesting and make us special.

Make your child aware that her coloring is unique to her, and that this uniqueness can be a source of personal pride. Discover and compare the similarities and differences in the coloring of the skin tones and facial features of each member of your family. Does your child have dark brown eyes like Dad? High cheekbones like Mom? Freckles like her sister? Or does she have physical traits that resemble other family members she cares about?

Look through magazines with your child and find pictures of people who have hair that is similar to her hair in color, texture, or style, or eyes of similar shape and color. Follow up on this activity by pointing out the beauty and variety of colors in other living things such as birds, fish, and animals.

Personal Space

Everyone needs privacy, and your child is no exception.

Give your child some personal space by identifying places in your home that are special safe places for him to play, read, store personal treasures, and be alone. This not only helps foster responsibility, but it also helps him develop a willingness to cooperate in shared family spaces. Your child will be proud to see his space in your home identified with his name and his self-portrait or photo. Personalize his bedroom door, his part of a closet, his toy chest, his desk, and his favorite chair, as well as his books, his clothes, his toothbrush, and his special toys. Give him art supplies of his very own, and keep them in a shoebox with his photo on the lid. Help your child label it with his name and the words "Art Box."

Sexuality

The question is not whether, but how well, you will teach your child about her sexuality.

A very important part of your child's attitudes about herself include her sexual identity. Children begin to learn positive sexual attitudes from the moment they are born, through feeding, skin-to-skin touching, cuddling, bathing, and massaging. Perpetuate these positive sexual attitudes by being natural and calm about her interest in her body, or in your body when you are in the bathroom, dressing, undressing, or wearing fewer clothes in hot weather. Try to react positively and objectively when she wants to look at other children's bodies to see how they differ.

To enable your child to grow up with a healthy attitude about her body and the sexual feelings which are a basic and a natural part of life, you need to be willing to answer honestly all of her questions about her body or sex. Let her know that you want her to feel good about her sexuality and gender, and that you are open to any questions she may want to ask.

Consult your local bookstore or library for more information about sexuality and how to teach it positively to your child.

What Is a Friend?

Friends are beautiful flowers in the garden of life.

When you talk to your child about friendships, let him know that a friendship is a responsibility.

Friends make each other feel good. They talk and listen to each other; take turns; share toys, ideas, interests, and feelings; and laugh and have fun together. Friends don't say mean things about each other and they care about what happens to each other. Friends can be of all ages and sizes. They may look different from you and from each other, but that's OK. Friends will have other friends besides you, and you can have as many or as few friends as you want.

Making Friends

Teaching your child to make friends is important in a world where people change jobs and locations frequently.

Making friends is a learned social skill; children are not born with it. Although some children make friends more easily than others, this is a skill that any child can learn or improve upon. You can help your child learn how to make and keep friends by encouraging her to practice the following strategies.

- Smile and greet others by name.
- Share and take turns.
- Be interested in what others are doing and ask them questions.
- Give compliments that you really mean.
- Listen carefully and look into the eyes of others when they speak.
- Stick up for those who are already your friends and say good things about them.

Making New Connections

Look for ways to help your child form new connections whenever your family moves.

If your family is uprooted and has to move away, your child will need to learn how to make new connections with others. Even if you keep in close touch with old friends, making new connections and participating in new groups is never a wasted effort. These are life skills that you can teach your child through your modeling and encouragement.

Join religious or community groups and involve your child in their activities. Take your child with you to help out when you volunteer for neighborhood or community events. Help him make friends through a child care center, your neighborhood, or a play group you start yourself. Encourage his interest in activities that will help him meet new friends and feel connected to various groups.

Expressing Yourself

Self-confidence stems from the security of feeling lovable and capable.

In order to make and keep friends, your child will need the confidence and ability to communicate her needs to other people. Some children are naturally outspoken, but if your child is shy about speaking around other people, she may need help practicing this skill.

Help your child become aware of her body language and facial expressions as she speaks. Demonstrate how much easier it is to talk to someone and ask questions if you look that person in the eye instead of looking at the floor.

Try not to assume or guess in advance what your child wants. Instead, ask her to tell you. When you're with her, don't speak for her, but ask her if she would like to do the telling. Make it clear that it's all right to speak up politely to tell others if she needs something at home, at school, or anywhere else.

Playing With Friends

Help your child plan cooperative games and activities to enjoy when friends come to play.

When your child plays with friends, encourage games that foster cooperation rather than competition. Also, plan activities in which everyone participates and is a "winner." Below are a few suggestions.

- Take a nature walk and collect moss, stones, seed pods, and twigs to glue onto individual pieces of wood or cardboard.
- Together, hold on to the edges of an old sheet and wave it up and down while the children take turns running under it.
- Act out a favorite story such as "The Three Little Pigs" or "Goldilocks and the Three Bears."
- Make a snack together and eat it.
- Make modeling dough together and play with it.
- Make and decorate cookies to give to a neighbor.
- Attach pictures to craft sticks to make puppets, and have a puppet show.
- Use crayons or markers to make a mural on a roll of paper or several large sheets of paper taped together.

How to Teach Sharing

With persistence and patience, you can teach your child to share.

Young children need to learn that some things are their own (a blanket or special stuffed animal) and do not have to be shared unless they are willing. Other toys or materials are things we share with brothers, sisters, and/or visiting friends.

A few of these are outside play equipment, the sandbox, blocks, books, and homemade modeling dough.

Help your child take turns by saying, "You've had a long turn to play with that. Let your brother have a turn now, and later you can have another turn." Or, "We have lots of crayons and paper. You can use the blue crayon while she uses the red one, and then you can trade." Or, "He doesn't have any modeling dough. You have a really big pile; can you please give him some of yours so that everyone can play?" Or, "You can take turns with the bucket and shovel, and while you wait for your turn you can use this can and big spoon. Then you can trade."

When children know they have not lost total ownership of a toy or a material and that there is time for everyone to have a turn, they become more comfortable with the idea of sharing.

Stages of Play

Recognize and celebrate your child's stages of play.

Children do not learn overnight or at a certain age to have friends and play cooperatively. They go through stages as described below. Think of these stages as milestones in your child's social development.

- *Solitary Play* (Infant to Toddler)

  Your child plays alone with her toys, fingers, and feet. She observes other children playing, but does not interact.

- *Parallel Play* (Toddler to 3 years)

  Your child plays next to another child, or even with the same pile of blocks, but does not interact with the child.

- *Cooperative Play* (3½ to 5 years)

  Your child starts to interact with others in small groups as they use toys and materials. She begins to learn how to share and take turns. Gradually, she learns to play with others and to start building skills in communicating, negotiating, and compromising.

Some children move through these stages faster than others, but don't worry about speed. Instead, help your child by encouraging positive interactions at whatever stage she has reached.

Feeling Capable

Basic Information

Teach your child basic information about herself and where she lives.

Reassure your child that if she is separated from you, lost, or in need of help, being able to give basic information about herself to an adult will help solve the problem.

Fear or stress may make your child forget, so pretend it is a memory game, and practice with her until she's learned the information by rote and it's as easy for her to do as breathing. Have her recite this information to other adults such as friends, teachers, and relatives, both in person when you aren't in the room and over the telephone. Discreetly label the inside of your child's tote, lunchbox, and coat with this information and make her aware of what these labels mean. It's important that your child can relate the following information.

- Her full name
- Her parents' names
- Her home address and phone number (including area code)
- The full name of a trusted friend, neighbor, or guardian
- The name of her school or day care

Following Directions

Whenever you ask your child to do something, you teach him to follow directions.

When your child enters school, he will need to listen to and remember directions with several parts ("Close your book, stand up, and come to the door") and do them in order. To practice this skill at home, play directions games with your child. Make up silly, sequential directions such as "Take off one shoe, put it on your head, and then clap your hands." Let your child give you silly directions, too. He will continue to practice this memory skill as he watches you follow his directions.

Safe in Public

Teach your child simple safety techniques.

When you visit public places such as parks, shopping centers, libraries, and grocery stores with your child, make his safety a priority. Set clear rules about staying close, looking but not touching, and being polite to, but wary of, strangers. Consider these public safety tips.

- Teach your child to stay where he is if he gets lost. He is never to walk toward exits or wander out into the parking lot if he can't find you.
- Set up a safety drill in your home in which you and your child make believe that you have been separated at a store. Pretend that you are a store employee, and have your child practice asking you for help.
- Try to avoid shopping or attending events when your child is tired, hungry, or ill. He will not be able to think clearly about his safety.
- Help your child identify people who can help him if he gets lost. Familiarize him with places such as cash registers, information booths, and service desks where store employees are likely to be found. Point out uniforms, name tags, badges, and special hats that set service employees apart from the general public.

Fire Safety

Make sure that your child has a healthy respect for the destructive potential of matches, lighters, and open flames.

Talk about and role-play fire safety with your child. Focus on fire safety practice as a game of pretend, but make it clear that the skills you are teaching him will keep him safe in case of a real fire emergency. Your practice drills should include tips for preventing smoke inhalation such as keeping low to the ground where the air is easier to breathe, as well as the following.

- Practice dialing 911 with the phone unplugged.
- Practice using the "stop, drop, and roll" technique in case his clothes catch on fire.
- Locate the fire extinguisher in your home and demonstrate how it is used.
- Develop several fire escape plans.
- Locate your smoke alarms and let him hear what they sound like.
- Take a tour of your local fire station and ask for free safety posters, pamphlets, stickers, and activity coloring books.
- Emphasize the importance of getting out of the house rather than hiding from a fire.

Gun Safety

Knowing what to do around a gun is a safety skill that may save your child's life.

Handguns and firearms in the home pose a grave danger to children. If you own a firearm, it is your responsibility to put a gun lock on the trigger, and keep the gun safely locked away. Consider carrying the key to your gun cabinet or case on a keychain, belt, or necklace. If you are wearing or carrying the key, you will know where it is at all times, and this will prevent your child from gaining access to it. For extra insurance against accidents, teach your child about firearm safety. Educate her about guns not to instill fear, but to increase a realistic understanding of their dangers.

Here are four basic rules that your child should follow if she finds or sees a gun.

- Stop.
- Don't touch.
- Leave the area.
- Tell an adult.

Safe Inside

Enable your child to learn and practice ways to be safe on his own.

Hopefully you will never need to leave your young child unattended. However, in case of an emergency, your child should know how to stay safe in your home. Designate a childproof room or rooms for him to play in if circumstances prevent you from keeping a close eye on him. Teach him the following safety tips, and make sure that your child knows why they are important.

- Stay inside the house at all times.
- Keep all doors and windows locked.
- Never open the door to anyone but immediate family members.
- Never tell anyone that you are alone.
- Call 911 if you are afraid.
- Don't answer the telephone.
- Set up a system of alerting close neighbors when there's an emergency, such as tying a red ribbon on your doorknob or hanging an ornament in a window.
- Be aware of all exits in case of fire.

Good Listener

Notice and listen to sounds both inside and outside.

Here are a few games that will encourage your child to listen more effectively.

- Always model good listening yourself! Your child will learn the most from your modeling.
- Encourage your child to make sounds for you to guess.
- Help your child make sounds with objects found around your house such as kitchen utensils, jar lids, bottle caps, tea balls, straws, and crumpled paper.
- Make a game of closing your eyes, listening carefully, and trying to point in the direction of a specific sound source.
- Make a sound matching game by placing small items such as buttons, paper clips, coins, and dried beans in pairs of empty plastic film containers. Tape the lids securely closed. Have your child shake the containers to find the pairs with the matching sounds.

Natural Disasters

Controlling a make-believe storm during pretend play will help your child stay calm during a real one.

If you live in an area where tornados, hurricanes, or other weather emergencies occur, be sure to practice with your child what to do. Talk about what happens during these storms, and choose a safe place to wait them out, such as a bathroom, closet, cellar, or basement. Being prepared gives your child a plan of action in the event of a storm watch. Let your child help you prepare a natural disaster kit with a working flashlight, batteries, matches, bandages, a can opener, a Swiss army knife, and enough food and water to keep everyone in your family fed for three days.

Create a pretend storm by showing your child how to drum her fingers on a tabletop for rain sounds and by howling and blowing to simulate wind. Shake a large aluminum roasting pan for thunder crashes, and use a flashlight for lightning. Make the storm sounds get louder and louder, and then let them fade away so that your child experiences the storm as it approaches and passes on. If she is afraid of storms, this kind of pretend practice will ease her fears about them, because when she pretends, she can control the storm's intensity.

Accepting Praise

Praise helps children only if they have learned to react to it positively.

Some children have difficulty accepting praise because it makes them feel self-conscious. Children who have problems accepting praise graciously may begin to discount the praise they receive and believe they are unworthy of it. Teach your child how to accept a compliment with a response that feels comfortable to him. Explain that if he's not sure he understands or really agrees with someone's praise, he can still say, "Thank you for saying that" or "Thank you, I'm glad you like it."

Encourage him to generate a response, even if he's still shy about it. With time, he'll gain the confidence to respond to praise in a more genuine way.

Establishing Routines

It's important to follow regular routines and rituals each day.

Establishing some continuity in your family life is important to your child's well-being. If your child attends a day-care center or a preschool, find out how naps, snacktime, and outside play times are scheduled so that you can coordinate this schedule with your weekend and after-care activities. If you can, try to eat meals together at about the same time each day. Try even harder to establish regular bedtime hours and a nightly bedtime routine. Consistent bedtime routine will give your child a sense of security that will help her sleep better. Make bedtime a sharing time by reading together or making a healthy bedtime snack with her on a regular basis.

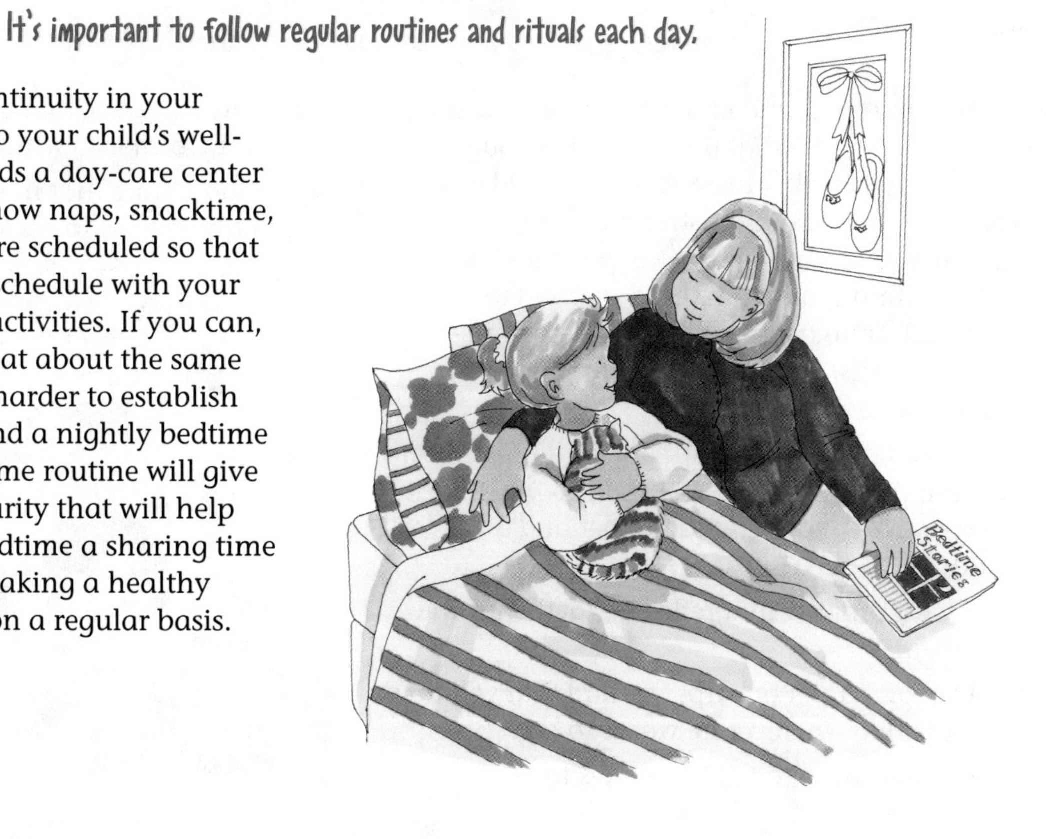

Security Objects

Favorite dolls or blankets are important to the emotional stability of your child.

Many young children find it easier to deal with their feelings if they have the comfort and reassurance of a favorite blanket, doll, or stuffed animal. If your child uses a security object, respect this behavior as a genuine need and a positive step in his emotional growth. Some children need their security objects most of the day; others use them only when they feel vulnerable, such as with new people, in new surroundings, or at bedtime. Let your child keep his security objects until he is ready to give them up. If you give him free rein to indulge this need, he will eventually gain the confidence and independence to outgrow it. Sometimes the responsibility of a pet, such as a guinea pig, a puppy, or a kitten, can help ease this transition.

Puppets and Props

Sometimes special tools are needed to help children share their feelings.

Hand puppets and other props create a safe, make-believe zone that provides just enough distance from reality to enable your child to feel less vulnerable about his strong feelings. Children who are just learning how to express their feelings may also find that it's easier to respond to puppets than to people. With the help of the following tools, it may be easier for your child to open up to you.

- A hand puppet that talks for your child (keep a puppet on hand for yourself, too, so that it can answer your child's puppet and give advice and reassurance)
- A magic mirror that reflects exactly how he feels inside
- A magic carpet or carpet square that will take your child wherever he wants to go
- A magic lamp to tell his wishes to
- A bottle filled with a magic potion that can change him into whatever he wants to be
- A magic cape that makes your child invisible, but gives voice to his secret feelings
- Face puzzles, masks, or dolls whose faces he can manipulate to reflect his mood

Individual Interests

Interests and hobbies help children stay emotionally fit.

Your child's interests will grow and change with time. However, it's important to encourage and nurture them as they appear. The individual interests that she develops outside of home, day care, or preschool will help put balance and enjoyment in her life both now and in the years to come, and enable her to form friendships with children with like interests.

Be aware of what your child enjoys. If, for example, she's thrilled by trains, take her on a train ride, read books about trains, and let her help you design a train birthday cake. The support, enthusiasm, and guidance that you provide will give her the courage to risk and explore further avenues of interest.

Death and Loss

Young children sometimes fear that they might be left alone or abandoned.

Children often experience loss and loneliness when parents are away at work or on a trip. But when a special loved one moves far away or dies, your child's loneliness may be mixed with the fear and anxiety that you might go away, too, and not come back. At such times you must be especially aware of your child's need for security. Let her know where you are at all times. Call her if you are apart, and give her extra comfort when you are together. If you are honest about your own feelings of sadness, it will help her know that you understand and share her feelings. Tangible tokens of your love, including your photo and special family symbols, will help your child feel less lonely when you are not together, and focusing on happy memories will help her gradually accept the loss.

Feeling OK About Being Imperfect

Fear of Failure

Children who are expected to always be perfect often develop fragile self-esteem.

Some children, particularly those of successful parents, are reluctant to risk making mistakes. They believe that if you can't be sure you'll do things perfectly, it's better not to try them at all. The mistakes themselves are less damaging than the belief that a mistake can make you a failure. If you have a child who feels this way, you may actually need to teach her to take small risks and make errors so that she will learn that mistakes are not tragic. Your child needs to know that she can fail and still be loved. She needs to accept mistakes as a necessary part of being human and to know that they don't detract from her overall competency. When your child makes a mistake, try emphasizing all of the things she did right.

- "You can tell me if you goofed; I've made lots of mistakes today, too."
- "I know you feel bad about the broken cup, but it's OK. It could happen to anyone."
- "You did lots of things right today. Let's talk about them instead."

Make a Mess

Make equal room for messiness and order in your home.

Every so often, making a big mess with your child will take the pressure off him to always be tidy both inside and outside your home. Try some of the activities below. If you control the where, what, and when of these activities, they'll be a source of shared laughter and good memories.

- Play in mud puddles on a spring day.
- Make mud pies and cookies and "bake" them on the front porch.
- Squirt unscented shaving cream into the bathroom sink and decorate the bathroom mirror.
- Fingerpaint with whipped cream or pudding.
- Make homemade modeling dough on the kitchen table.
- Write on your tub and tiles with soap crayons.

Be Realistic

Unreasonable expectations are a heavy burden.

Young children need to explore their environment with their whole bodies, so getting dirty is part of their daily work and play. If your child is never allowed to get dirty or make a mess, she may develop the unhealthy and unrealistic attitude that she must always be "perfect." Keep this in mind when you dress your child for everyday play activities. Don't expect her to stay perfectly clean and unrumpled even if she's dressed in her Sunday best for a special event.

Provide your child with clothes that are sturdy, machine washable, and which allow for freedom of movement. Teach her a few simple but consistent rules about where to take off her shoes, where to put her dirty clothes, and when and how to clean herself up. If your child attends a child-care facility or a preschool, or when she visits family or friends, be sure to bring along at least one complete change of clothing, just in case.

Helpful Criticism

If focused on helping, not hurting, criticism can promote an inner sense of responsibility.

Constructive criticism is a way to help your child change his behavior or improve at an activity without making him feel bad about himself. Offer positive suggestions for improving his performance, and involve him in finding ways to do things differently. For example, if he's playing in the water instead of actually washing the dishes, you might say, "Sometimes I like to make mounds out of soapsuds too, and you've made some really big ones, but that took a long time. If you use these soapsuds on the dishes and put them here to rinse, we can finish this job quickly. Then we'll have time to play outside."

Invite your child to think of other ways to keep jobs fun while still getting the work done. This kind of problem solving will teach him how to take responsibility for his behavior and become personally involved in improving it.

Sharing Feelings

Reassure your child that all of her feelings are valid.

Create a sharing time each day to help your child talk about her feelings. Try to choose a quiet time of the day when she is settled and less distracted, perhaps after supper or just before bedtime. Take the lead by sharing some of the emotions that you felt during the day. Then invite your child to talk about her day. Let her know that it's OK for her to have both positive and negative feelings.

- "I felt tired and sad when I got home from work because it seemed like such a long day and I missed you."
- "How did you feel when the sun came out today? I felt very happy about it."
- "I was worried when I drove to the store with you because there was ice and snow on the road."
- "I had fun making pizza with you this evening. How did you feel about helping me cook?"

Memories

Tell stories about how you handled mistakes when you were a child.

Making mistakes is a big part of learning and growing. An important step in your development as a parent is to honor the mistakes you've made in the past and to let your children have room to make mistakes of their own. If you're reluctant to admit your mistakes, then your child may be intimidated by his perception that you're perfect. He may then find it difficult to acknowledge his own mistakes or talk to you about them.

Encourage your child to feel more comfortable with mistakes by talking about the mistakes you made when you were his age. Discuss how you felt about them at the time, and how you overcame them and learned from them. Above all, make it clear that your love for him doesn't lessen when he makes mistakes. Let him know he can turn to you when he's troubled or in trouble.

She's Just Shy

All of us are shy in some situations and outgoing in others.

Try not to make assumptions or label your child as shy or outgoing, introverted or extroverted. Generalizing could lead you to expect a certain kind of behavior of her, or to expose her to certain experiences and not to others. It also can give her an incorrect perception of herself. For example, some children who are labeled shy are very strong-willed and persistent individuals. When they watch others on the playground or wait for a rowdy group in line to disperse, they are being observant, not shy.

Some children become drained when they interact with or talk to others. They need personal space to be alone in and time to relax and recharge. Other children get recharged from interacting with others, and don't work well alone. Some children are very careful about what they share with you because sharing is giving up a piece of themselves. Others share everything with anyone, with no misgivings. To nurture positive attitudes in your child, accept her individual qualities without labeling, and help her identify as individual strengths her unique ways of handling situations.

Gifts and Gift Ideas

Making gifts for others fosters generosity and teaches your child the joy of giving.

Make homemade gifts a family tradition, not only at holiday time but any time that gift giving is appropriate. When children make gifts, they learn the good feeling of giving something of themselves to others. Gather and save materials beforehand and arrange some space and time for making the gifts together with your child. You can help him make gifts any time of the year—on summer days when you may have extra time for this kind of family fun, or on rainy days when he needs something to do. Let your child wrap and label the gifts so that they are ready when you need them.

The ideas that follow are easy gifts that you and your child can make together. Try one or more of them. If you wish, let your child make gift-wrap by using thick, colorful tempera paint to stamp handprints on tissue paper or cut-open brown paper bags.

- Placemats—Cut shapes from construction paper, gift-wrap, and aluminum foil. Let your child glue the shapes on large pieces of construction paper. Laminate the papers or cover them with clear self-stick paper.
- Stationery—Make a stamp by cutting a design in the end of a potato. Let your child dip the stamp in paint and press it on pieces of note paper to make prints.
- "I Love You" Book—Have your child tell you what he loves best about a friend or a relative. Write down these thoughts in a blank book and let your child illustrate the pages with crayons or markers.

Little Things Mean a Lot

Doing everyday things together as a family will mean the most to your child.

It is not the big, annual vacation that does the most to promote a sense of belonging in the family; it's the ongoing "little things." Below are some small—but important—ways you can help promote feelings of family togetherness for your child.

- Work together on family projects such as making a bird feeder, washing the car, or having a garage sale.
- Make spaghetti together.
- Go on family picnics.
- Schedule family movie nights.
- Work on scrapbooks or photo albums together.

Family Games

Foster cooperation skills by playing family games in which your child can participate.

Many families enjoy playing cards or board games together. Try very simple table games with 3- and 4-year-olds such as sorting game pieces by size or color, but don't be afraid to try teaching more challenging games to 4- to 5-year-olds, such as matching cards or dominoes. Play games in which your child can participate and that all ages can enjoy.

For instance, after dinner you could play a progressive-story game in which each person tells just a little of a made-up story and then passes the story on to the next person, who adds to it. Or try the word game called If. To play, ask each person a question such as "If you could be an animal, which one would you be and why?" or "If you could be anyone on TV, who would you be and why?" or "If you could travel anywhere, where would it be and why?" Together, make up your own games to play as a family.

Taping Elders' Stories

Keeping family stories alive is a great way to strengthen togetherness.

One of the easiest ways to preserve your family history is to tape-record the stories of parents, grandparents, or great-grandparents. Plan a time to do this, and do it casually, without fanfare, when older relatives visit you. Ask them to tell about such things as their funniest experiences, their childhood games, or what they did on weekends when they were little. Tape their stories about going to school, their first job, their most embarrassing moment, or how they met their spouse. Follow up by making a tape that tells about when your child was born or about how you and your child's other parent met. These stories will become invaluable ties to the family for your child. They are part of your family's history and her heritage.

Family Scrapbooks

Making family scrapbooks is a perfect activity for promoting togetherness.

Family scrapbooks can increase your child's sense of belonging in two ways. First, when helping to make the scrapbooks, he will work with other family members to save, sort, arrange, and glue the scrapbook items. Second, he will gain a sense of family togetherness when he looks at completed or in-progress scrapbooks and recalls memories of times past with you.

Designate a few shoeboxes or baskets as holders for saving items such as photos, ticket stubs, postcards from travels, newspaper clippings, school play programs, or wedding and birth announcements. Plan a regular time, at least once a month, to work on the scrapbooks. If you wish, make separate scrapbooks for family camping experiences, family trips, activities with friends, birthdays, holidays, family reunions, and so on. Keep the scrapbooks in a place where you and your child can look at them often.